The Xenophobe's® Guide to The Icelanders

Richard Sale

Oval Books

Published by Oval Books
335 Kennington Road
London SE11 4QE
United Kingdom

Telephone: +44 (0)20 7582 7123
Fax: +44 (0)20 7582 1022
E-mail: info@ovalbooks.com
Web site: www.xenophobes.com

First published by Ravette Books, 1994

First published by Oval Books 2000
Revised and updated 2001, 2003

Editor – Catriona Tulloch Scott
Series Editor – Anne Tauté

Cover designer – Jim Wire, Quantum
Printer – Cox & Wyman Ltd
Producer – Oval Projects Ltd

Acknowledgement and thanks are given to:

William Jón Holm for the use of his poem
'The Icelandic Language', also published in a
different translation in *The Dead Get By With
Everything* by Milkwood Editions (USA), 1991.

Xenophobe's® is a Registered Trademark.

ISBN: 1-902825-32-2

Contents

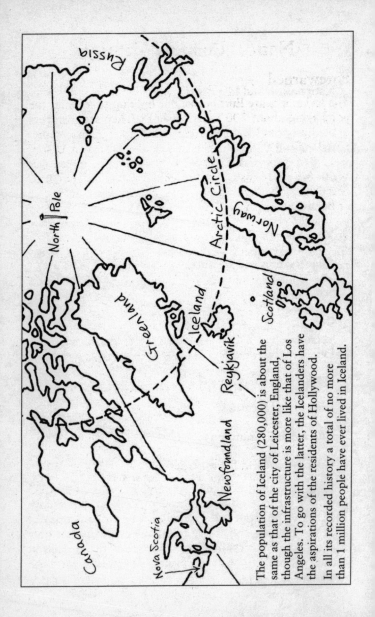

The population of Iceland (280,000) is about the same as that of the city of Leicester, England, though the infrastructure is more like that of Los Angeles. To go with the latter, the Icelanders have the aspirations of the residents of Hollywood.

In all its recorded history a total of no more than 1 million people have ever lived in Iceland.

Nationalism and Identity

Forewarned

The Icelanders are Europeans, but only up to a point, the point lying about 200 miles offshore. They are members of the European Economic Area and of E.F.T.A., and sometimes think they would like to join the European Union, feeling that they have a huge contribution to make. But there are problems. It is difficult for the Icelanders to accept that they would not have the same voting power as, say, the British and the Germans. When it is pointed out that there are very few of them in comparison, they do not understand. One country, one vote, surely?

But the Icelanders' real concern is fishing. Cod is the basis of their economy and they are nervous of foreign trawlers ruining their livelihood. One of the reasons they like the British is because they lost the last Cod War. It was a friendly war and the Icelanders like losers, as long as they lose to Iceland that is.

Icelanders are proud of the fact that their country is unique. Nowhere else are there lava deserts, active volcanoes and icecaps. At the same time they recognise that as a nation they are tiny and of limited standing in the world. The insecurity this creates makes the Icelanders, a very close-knit nation with a developed sense of community, behave as though they were indeed the centre of the universe. It seems absolutely right to them that when Jules Verne sent his travellers to the centre of the earth, it was down through an Icelandic volcano.

It was recently discovered that in the winter of 1002/1003 Snorri Thorfinnsson was born in Vinland (nowadays believed to be either Newfoundland or Nova Scotia) of Icelandic parents, the first non-Indian American. It is only a matter of time before the Icelanders file a lawsuit claiming North America on behalf of Snorri's surviving relatives.

How They See Themselves

A few years ago the Icelanders suffered a shock when blood-typing suggested that they might be of Gaelic, rather than Viking, stock. To have the same roots as the Americans (who are basically Irish and therefore quite beyond the pale), and even to share characteristics with the English (who are amiable enough but arrogant), was almost more than could be borne. As it was known (but kept very quiet) that when the Vikings arrived there were already Irish monks in Iceland, some historians suggested that there had actually been an Irish settlement and that the Vikings had either killed all the settlers or, much worse, interbred with them. It is now thought that the few monks who got there first left in disgust at having to share their sanctuary with heathens, and that the blood results could be explained away by natural causes or, better still, by the suggestion that the Vikings kidnapped a few Gaelic women from the Shetlands or Orkneys on the way. The national psyche has been restored to health.

Icelanders hold themselves in the very highest esteem. They are the sons of Vikings, the greatest of all ancient races, renowned for their strength, fortitude, good looks and masculine values. The fact that these same ancestors are also famous for rape and pillage is discreetly ignored, as is their somewhat dubious attitude towards women. Icelanders are also reluctant to talk about Ingólfur, the first Viking to land on Iceland. As a mark of respect they have named the spot where he landed Ingólfshöfði, but they put it in small print on their maps so that as few people as possible notice that it is merely a knob of rock some three miles out to sea.

As proof of their innate superiority Icelanders point out that Iceland is the navel of the world. If you doubt the veracity of this claim you need only consult the Viking Sagas, the greatest of all literary achievements, where this view is expressed countless times during the course of long meandering tales of murder and revenge.

They point out that they have the biggest and best of many things. They have Vatnajökull, the largest glacier in Europe, with an area almost as large as Cyprus, which makes France's Mer de Glace look like an ice cube by comparison. Their waterfalls are higher, more powerful and more beautiful than any others in Europe. And even if Strokkur, their only surviving geyser, is smaller than the one in America's Yellowstone National Park, they are able to remind you that it can be found at Geysir, the Icelandic name now used to describe all such natural gushing phenomena. They also have the most westerly point in Europe, a place guaranteed to annoy the Irish who have erected numerous signs in Dingle claiming the same thing.

Even the Icelandic pony gets in on the act, having five gaits rather than the four favoured by the rest of the world's horses.

Icelanders see themselves as cultured and sophisticated, with an enviable literary heritage and independence of spirit. These points are always included in speeches by their presidents, who are seen as the embodiment of the nation and whose comments are quoted as gospel and prefaced with a friendly "As the president says…". In fact, so often is this phrase used that it has become a kind of valediction.

How They See Others

It might be imagined that the Icelanders, sharing a mutual Viking heritage with the Scandinavian nations, would see them as brothers. Not so. Their isolation has meant that they still speak the language of the Vikings while the rest of the Scandinavians speak an inferior tongue comprising low German and a mishmash of other bits and pieces.

The Norwegians are laughed at for their enthusiasm

for outdoor pursuits which is looked on as proof of what the Icelanders thought anyway, that the Norwegians are slow-witted and dull. Ask the Icelanders about the paintings of Munch, the music of Grieg and the books of Hamsun and they will tell you it is likely these individuals were descended from Icelandic Vikings who went home for the weekend and were stranded by a recalcitrant tide or wind. The discovery of North Sea oil and the fact that it has made the Norwegians very rich has led to a change of view. Now the Norwegians are seen as slow-witted, dull, and quite disgustingly lucky.

The Swedes are considered to be self-centred, sex-mad and too frequently given to bouts of pleasure seeking – indulgences rather too close to their own not to resent them for it.

Norwegians and Swedes are also disapproved of for being Arctic nations. With its name and its wild landscape Iceland might be expected to lie within the Arctic Circle, but only the island of Grimsey off the northern coast manages to do so, and then only by a few yards. As a consequence, Icelanders deride the Circle and say that only one man in Iceland can be bothered to cross it. He is the vicar of Grimsey and he only does so because the Circle runs through the centre of his bed.

The English are looked on as laughable and lovable eccentrics, much given to coming second. The Icelanders find this latter characteristic hilarious and strangely reassuring. Almost the whole population speaks English due to the presence of an American air-force base in Iceland which means that the nation is flooded with American television programmes. However, though they tune in all day to American television, they moan constantly about its poor quality and the effect it is having on the younger generation.

While the upstart Columbus gets the kudos for discovering the New World, the Icelanders revel in the knowledge that it was one of their own, Leifur Eríksson, who

8

did so several centuries before. Some now wish he hadn't: as Churchill is reputed to have said, 'The Icelanders had the good sense to forget they had discovered America'. Icelanders like American dollars, but rather resent the servicemen who spend them. To get their own back, they banished the Americans to an inhospitable, lonely corner of the island on the pretext that Iceland's only international airport (Keflavík) is there. Oddly, if you ask, they will claim that Keflavík lies in this wilderness because it was built close to where the Americans were.

Special Relationships

The Icelanders have a special relationship with the Danes but this has nothing to do with their common Viking origin. Until the early 20th century Denmark ruled Iceland which is why the Icelanders see the Danes as having exploited their country, keeping it poor and uneducated, primitive and isolated. The older generation have a saying: 'Danes make good rulers for Danes', which is a roundabout way of saying that they should stay at home with their LEGO. However an exception is made for any internationally famous Dane about whom older Icelanders can feel proprietorial.

Younger Icelanders are inclined to a different view of history. Danish is still taught in Icelandic schools (it was only replaced in 1998 by English as the primary foreign language), so youngsters develop an affinity with the Danes. They see them as cousins and can be wildly enthusiastic about them – as long as there are no Danes actually present.

The only other nations with which the Icelanders have any rapport are Luxembourgers, Canadians and Russians. Luxembourg has the largest community of Icelandic expatriots in Europe because until recently the European headquarters of Icelandair was situated there. Icelanders share with the Luxembourgers an inferiority complex born of being so few in number. The Icelanders and the Luxembourgers do not often score high points in the Eurovision Song Contest* and regularly lose at football (though individual Icelanders are making an impact in European leagues).

The Canadian connection is a family one. As many as 10,000 Icelanders emigrated to Canada in the 1880s, and ties have been maintained. When an Icelander meets a Canadian, the Canadian is expected to know the Canadian relatives of the Icelander he is speaking to.

The Russians are special for different reasons. Russian trawlers regularly dock and disgorge men of seemingly overwhelming stupidity who can be persuaded to exchange much-prized bottles of fierce vodka for clapped-out Ladas and other vehicles. Those who taste the vodka have no doubts about who has the better deal.

How They Would Like Others to See Them

They wish to be seen as they see themselves, as a highly cultured race. As proof of their sophistication, Icelanders are able to point to the publication of a monthly English-language newspaper. How many other countries produce a paper in a language other than their own? Its writers even use colloquialisms to prove their grasp of English. The paper is indeed impressive; it doesn't much matter that the mix of cliché and dated slang makes it quite clear that it has not been written by someone whose first language is English.

---

* For this they are quite grateful. The Icelandic economy could not survive winning and having to stage the next event. Indeed, if it wasn't for the fact that the Norwegians appear to have a monopoly on last place, the Icelanders would favour the view that coming last was the only sensible course.

Character

Strength and Intelligence

The Vikings who settled Iceland in 870 were folk who could not tolerate the order imposed on their Scandinavian homelands by the king who had unified the countries. That independent disposition is still an Icelandic characteristic: the Icelander is an individualist and an adventurer.

The country also imposed itself on the national character. Those early settlers had a hard time. Then the climate eased and by the mid 12th century there was spare time to devote to fighting. Three groups of islanders fought on and off for nearly a century, a time now known as the 'Age of Sturlungar' from Sturla, a farmer from north of Reykjavík who was the father of Snorri Sturluson, one of Iceland's greatest poets, the author of *Egil's saga*. (It is said that Snorri maintained a herd of 120 cattle solely to produce the calves on whose skins he wrote his stories.)

After the Age of Sturlungar the climate worsened which made fighting impossible: everyone's energy was consumed by staying alive. But the harsh, dark winters meant that the farmers had little to do but read and relate the sagas. This created a literate, artistically minded people.

Their history gives rise to the dual personality of the Icelander. He values both his artistic heritage and his hardiness. The nation has survived appalling natural catastrophes; in 1783-5 the largest volcanic eruption the world has ever seen occurred killing a quarter of the population when the 'Haze of Hunger' (dust from the eruption) blocked out the sun. But the inhabitants shrugged it off. Today's Icelander draws comfort from this. He wants an Icelandic man to be the world's strongest, yet also wishes to be seen as a highly cultured person divorced from menial daily tasks. When Jón Páll

Sigmarsson won the title of the world's strongest man he delighted all Icelanders during one part of the competition when he was required to lift a vast and improbable load above his head. As he raised it he said *"Ekkert mál fyrir Jón Páll"*. This translates as "No problem for John Paul", but in Icelandic it rhymes. The Icelanders were euphoric – Jón Páll had reinforced the national idea that the Icelander is a strong poet.

Not only has an Icelander held the title of World's Strongest Man, but there have been several Icelandic Miss Worlds. There have also been a surprising number of Icelandic chess grandmasters, and Iceland has more writers and artists per capita than any other country on earth. These facts reinforce the Icelanders' belief that they are a nation of strong, beautiful and intelligent people.

Self-sufficient and Social

The Icelander may be individualistic, but he is also an 'associated man', addicted to clubs and groups; most Icelanders go to one or two gatherings each week – such as those of the Club for Humorous Pranks, or the Club for Wine Tasters Provided That Inebriation Does Not Lead to Divorce. His enthusiasm for clubs does not extend as far as the joining of trades unions. He finds such organizations altogether too earnest.

The life of the solitary farmer or fisherman may have made the Icelander appear withdrawn and silent, even shy, but this is now changing, travel having broadened him into a more sociable individual.

The Icelander is a hard worker, but erratic. He is self-reliant, flexible and long-suffering, but self-conscious, immodest and impatient. He is generous with regard to his friends, but also self-centred. He has little enthusiasm for the achievements of others, no matter how tremendous, but is upset when his own achievements, however modest, are not greeted as earth shattering.

Icelandic women are strong-willed and self-sufficient, both qualities dating from the fishing tradition, when the women organised the home and farm and managed everything while waiting for their men to return; often the men did not.

Fishing communities have always had a high number of single mothers because of the shorter life expectancy of fathers. (There is still no social stigma attached to being a lone mother, married or otherwise. In fact, there are more single mothers than ever today and Iceland has the highest illegitimate birthrate in Europe.)

Since they have maintained their strength and independence, feminism is seen as a backward step, for why accept equality when you have superiority? It is somewhat surprising that the modern Icelandic woman marries the modern Icelandic man. The only battleground of the sexes is politics where strong-minded women feel they have suffered at the hands of weak-minded men for years.

The Farmer's Mentality

Iceland came very quickly into the 20th century. Having been an isolated, insular race until 1940, the Icelanders suddenly found themselves the centre of attention. Invaded (for their own good, or so they were told) by the British and Americans, they discovered that they were rich beyond their wildest dreams. New markets for their fish made them for many years the wealthiest nation in Europe. This happened to a simple country people, and rustic attitudes remained. It is said that in 1946 the Icelanders had the highest number of bath tubs per capita of any European country, but that more often than not their main use was for keeping fish fresh.

The average farmer is considered well able to solve most of life's problems given 20 minutes, a hammer and a piece of string. This belief was reinforced by the country's early road builders who were book-trained engineers and proved to be quite useless. Even when they got it right, the bridges they built to connect outlying parts of the country to the main roads became an object of scorn: once the folk they were built to serve had used them to migrate to the towns, the bridges fell into disrepair and disuse behind them.

Being new to the concept of town-dwelling, the Icelanders still find its rules difficult. If you have been used to riding into the nearest village and hitching your horse to a rail outside the shop you want to visit, you expect to be able to do the same with your car. As a consequence, the underground car park in Reykjavík remained empty while the streets were full of cars whose drivers studiously ignored the parking meters. To combat this, the city authorities introduced an army of formidable parking wardens. So good have they been at their job that no-one now parks in the city centre at all and several shops in Laugavegur (the main street) have been forced to close down. Even the authorities are said to pine for the old days, but nobody has the courage to tackle the wardens.

One custom has been maintained. If you are driving through town and see someone you know on the pavement or in a car coming the other way, you will stop for a chat, just as you would if you met him on horseback. Such conversations last as long as they last. If that is a very long time, and it often is, the queue of vehicles behind the talkers will soon be miles long. The Icelanders tolerate this behaviour up to a point. Those who become sufficiently irate might blow their horns, but if they do this, the offending motorists and everyone else within earshot will fix them with a withering stare. However, there is an up-side. If someone is trying to cross a road, particularly when loaded with parcels, drivers will give way.

Rural attitudes have had odd repercussions. Icelanders

made news some years ago by banning dogs from their towns. They told the world that the ban was due to problems with dog mess and the worms it carried. But the real reason was that the Reykjavík authorities thought dog-owning reeked too much of the rural past – the sophisticated town dweller didn't need a sheepdog.

Dog owning is now allowed again though the cost of a dog licence is extortionate to reinforce official disapproval.

Beliefs and Values

The Hold of the *Huldufólk*

Although it is not obvious to every visitor to the island, Iceland is inhabited by a whole host of folk besides the Icelanders. There are elves, who are about the size of ordinary people but mostly stay hidden from view. They live in hills. There are trolls. Unlike Norwegian trolls, the Icelandic troll is not small and ugly and does not live under a bridge in mortal fear of billy goats. Icelandic trolls are 10 to 12 feet tall and live in mountains. And there are dwarfs. Icelandic dwarfs are as tiny as might be expected and live in rocks. Collectively this army is known in Icelandic as *huldufólk* – hidden people, and their dwellings are easy to spot: they are exceptionally beautiful rocks, mountains and hills.

The visitor who thinks that all this is nonsense underestimates the hold the tales of hidden people have on the Icelandic mind. The landscape is so awesome that human beings cannot help but feel insignificant in relation to it. This was exacerbated by the early settlers living a life of solitude, well separated from their neighbours. (The farms had to be large as the soil was so poor.) Brought up on tales of the Viking past, of a world peopled with curious gods and superheroes, it is understandable that the Icelanders saw the land as the home of supernatural beings. Belief runs so deep it is difficult to separate myth and reality. The main road from Reykjavík to Selfoss bears left for no apparent reason a few miles beyond Hveragerði, near a church on the right. It does this in order to avoid an elf hill. Even now, town streets are aligned to avoid elf hills and dwarf rocks. Past experience has taught the people that to attempt to build over a *huldufólk* site is useless. Bulldozers will fail, hammers will break, nothing can be done to destroy the site, so you might just as well go round it.

Today's youngsters are still told stories of the hidden people and enjoy the tradition because it adds something to their view of nature. But it is real enough to suggest that the old pagan Viking roots are closer to the surface than many Icelanders would care to admit.

A great grandmother will have told of the time her sheep went missing for a few days and an elf woman came to her door to apologise, saying she had needed ewe's milk for her sick infant, and telling her where the sheep could be found.

At a public lecture about the *huldufólk*, when the speaker asked how many of the audience believed in elves, about 80% of those present raised their hands. Of them 50% had spoken to an elf and 25% had seen one. One man admitted to having made love to an elf (*álfur* in Icelandic) but it turned out he was hard of hearing and had thought the speaker had been talking about a calf (*kálfur*).

An Icelander living in Canada placed an advertisement in the national Icelandic newspaper. He wanted a female elf to go to Canada as companion to a male elf who had inadvertently travelled with a group of emigrating Icelanders. The male elf, starved of love and friendship, was making a nuisance of himself. The paper followed up the story hoping to join in the joke, but the advertiser wasn't joking, which probably didn't surprise the readers.

If you ask Icelanders about the hidden people you may well be told a story about Niels Bohr, the Danish physicist and Nobel prizewinner, with whom they feel a kinship since Iceland was under Danish rule when he was at the peak of his powers. At that time he used to have a lucky horseshoe hanging in his study. An incredulous visitor said that he found it hard to believe that so eminent a scientist could believe in such things. "Oh I don't," said Bohr, "but I'm told it works even if you don't believe in it."

Profit Before Protection

Having the last great wilderness in Europe, you would expect the Icelanders to be a green nation. This is not the case, at least not if green issues stand in the way of profit. But with the increasing importance of tourism to the economy there is a definite colour shift towards green. It is, after all, the colour of the American dollar.

The Icelanders have an ambivalent attitude towards nature. There are many National Parks set up to protect the best of the landscape, but a bounty is paid for shooting Arctic foxes, and there is an ongoing debate over the rights and wrongs of whaling. (The Icelandic expression for good luck is *hvelreki* which translates as 'May a whole whale wash up on your beach'.)

When the earliest settlers arrived in Iceland there were forests where now there are just mossy deserts. The trees were cut down for their longboats and soon there were no trees to speak of. There has been an attempt to create new woodland areas, but the climate means that trees grow slowly and are stunted by the wind. A national joke is that if you are lost in an Icelandic forest all you need do is stand up. Curiously for a country which has no trees, the Icelanders use wooden scaffolding which is attached to buildings by bits of string and electrical flex.

Wood is easier on the hands when winter temperatures plummet, though the attachment points appear to be chosen for their flimsy nature and only superficially attached to the building in question.

The lack of forests is ironical because one of the ways in which American soldiers, for whom Iceland was an unpopular posting, were encouraged to come to the island was to be told that there was a beautiful, blonde virgin beneath every tree.

Family Trees and Fortunes

The ancient kings of Iceland being Danish, there is no Icelandic aristocracy. In its absence, and since the Icelanders have realised that there are no classless societies in Europe, several 'classes' are developing.

One of the more interesting used to be a class based on family history. Since few families could trace their family back more than a few generations, those that could were proud of being able to point out that their ancestors had been the occupants of the first longboats to be drawn up on the southern beaches. But recently a vast database using information from the Sagas, church registers and census returns has allowed everyone to do the same. The result is that almost every Icelander now knows he is related to his next-door neighbour in some way. As a consequence the word 'uncle' is now used as a term of mutual description, for if you go back far enough it is probably true.

The new database has stirred further interest in the Vikings, and a book has been published on their sayings. It is a remarkably fat book in view of the fact that history suggests they only used two phrases, i.e., (to a man) "Take that", and (to a woman) "Take this".

Another class is education-based, and 'ill-educated' is an increasingly derogatory term. This is odd because the Icelanders have an abiding suspicion of education. Useful subjects in particular, such as science, engineering and languages, are not deemed to be worth studying. On the other hand, they are impressed by lawyers and doctors, and are also very fond of philosophers. A poor philosopher stands higher on the social scale than a technician or a good plumber, with the result that on occasions neither Icelandic theories nor Icelandic pipes hold water.

The most significant class is based on money. In this the Icelanders are no different from other nations, though enthusiasm for believing that the rich are a better class is taken to extremes. The rich must be better – they have a house abroad and a big car.

The Icelander is impressed by others' financial fortune, but jealous of it. Any show of wealth is met by a public sneer – implying a dislike of ostentation – but a private grinding of teeth. In Iceland it is best to make your money quickly, before anyone knows what you're doing. Money, or the lack of it in comparison to others, causes great stress, and it is remarkable that life expectancy is still rising, rather than falling like a stone.

The Icelander's attitude to social standing is illustrated by the following story. Very early one morning some fishermen were making their way down to the shore for a day's fishing. They passed a house and as they did so the door opened and out came a group of professional men. A lawyer and a doctor, both unsteady on their feet, were carrying the paralytic form of the local mayor while a clergyman carried the mayor's hat. Seeing the fishermen, the group looked away, not because they were ashamed, but because in Icelandic society the professionals were of superior standing and would not dream of talking to rough fishing types. This story fits in neatly with the Icelandic view that those at the top of the social pile, while enviably rich, are either daft or drunkards.

Faith in Fate

Like most nationalities the Icelanders are very religious in a crisis. Otherwise they are one of the least religious societies in Europe. The fatalism that was bred of fishing and a harsh climate led them in the past to attribute sufferings to God's will. Today God has been removed from the equation, but similar reasoning allows the Icelander to assume that everyone's problems are their own fault. Except for his own, of course.

Obsessions

Politics and, in particular, the failings of politicians are a national obsession. But the chief obsession is:

The Weather

Icelanders are fond of saying that Iceland does not get real weather, just samples. They also say that if you don't like the weather you just have to wait five minutes and it will alter.

What they really mean is that since the island is sandwiched between cold Arctic air heading south, and warm Gulf Stream air flowing north, it is prone to rapid change. It is possible to experience all four seasons in one day – the speed of the change depending on the strength of the wind. Since the wind usually blows hard, a day that starts out badly, with rain and thick cloud, may be fine by midday. The Icelanders want the visitor to take heart from this. The problem is that if the weather is nice, all you have to do is wait five minutes and then it isn't.

Iceland is close enough to the Arctic Circle to see the midnight sun for several weeks in June and July. It is also close enough to experience several weeks in December and January when it does not get light at all. Winters are therefore rather more endured than enjoyed. People like the first snow because it heralds a white Christmas, but by February are sick of it and by April heartily sick of it. Spring never seems to come, and by the time it has finally arrived, autumn seems to be just around the corner.

Town dwellers mistreat the snow. It is ploughed, gritted, and generally abused until it ends up in dirty, sullen heaps at street corners and on the islands in the middle of the road where it gobbles up the boots of the unwary making crossing a road as hazardous as any expedition to the Pole. Just when the snow seems beaten, the daytime temperature rises and the heaps melt. But at nightfall it drops again and the whole wet mess freezes so that morning brings a pantomime of slipping people and sliding cars.

Sometimes this sequence is repeated for a week or more, by the end of which everyone is short tempered and near suicidal.

Trends and Hi Tech

The Icelanders have style.

They suffer a climate that is best described as miserable but they don't allow it to get in the way of wearing the trendiest garb. If this decrees open-toed sandals, then that is what they will wear, even if the snow is four feet deep.

Style is learned early. Stand outside any school and you will be treated to a show of the latest in world fashion. A recent survey of teenagers in Reykjavík – aimed at proving that Iceland has the highest usage of mobile phones in Europe – failed to find a single 16-year-old girl who did not have one.

People aspire to all the newest gadgets and gizmos, though this has as much to do with an obsession with technology and keeping up with the Magnussons as it has with style. If a new television model comes on the market it has to be purchased (and the old one can be put in the bedroom or kitchen). This overt materialism means that most Icelanders would almost prefer to live in a cardboard box than do without the latest hi-fi or electronic aid. But the box would be furnished and equipped to the highest standards.

Obsession with new technology means that the interior of the Icelandic house is state of the art, but in contrast the electrics and plumbing of most houses are a mess. Even the best-appointed homes will have a light fitting hanging off the ceiling and a leaking tap.

The Icelanders' enthusiasm for interiors is not translated to the exterior. The climate is harsh. Plants die quickly unless they are lovingly cared for, in which case they die slowly. Gardening has not caught on, which means that the only fad not to have been imported from Europe or America is the garden centre. The climate also destroys any attempt to keep the outside of buildings tidy, so that even the smartest hotels have concrete external walls, the concrete blotched like a modern art painting. Buildings are roofed with corrugated iron which is regularly painted to keep it rust and leak free. Bright colours are cheaper than pastel ones, so the cheapest and brightest are used. The towns and villages look as though they have been built by primary school children.

The obsession with the modern is in part a rejection of the Icelandic past and not everyone sees this as altogether a good thing. During a storm on the east coast, when high winds picked up a number of barbecues and deposited them out to sea, one commentator was moved to alter a well-known saying for bad weather – *'Það rignir eldi og eimyrju'* (It's raining fire and iron) – a saga reference to the heat of battle – to announce that it was raining fire and grills, a sardonic view of the 'suburbanisation' of the nation.

Style is expensive, but since it is essential to their way of life, Icelanders live on credit cards and borrowed money. Next to their cars and electronic gadgetry, their credit rating is the closest thing to the Icelanders' heart. Credit cards are accepted in all hotels and shops, down to the smallest kiosk. Indeed, if you just want a tube of toothpaste and offer a shop assistant cash, it will be assumed that you have no credit rating at all. You will be pointed out to other assistants and followed around. After all, if you have been reduced to using cash it is possible that you are a shoplifter.

It's a Bum Wrap

The other obsession is never mentioned. Icelanders are intimidated by toilet rolls, fearing that ownership of them might imply that the owner is less than perfect.

Before there were supermarkets in Iceland, toilet rolls used to be wrapped in anonymous brown paper and dropped discreetly out of sight into large shopping bags. Supermarkets have forced people to come clean, in a manner of speaking, but the obsession lives on.

Behaviour

The typical Icelander is quiet and restrained in the company of strangers. In any meeting he is the man who says nothing and is constantly amazed by those who ask questions. Special amazement is reserved for people who, like the Americans, are able to talk for an hour on a particular subject – two if they actually know anything about it. By contrast, the Icelander will have difficulty in filling five minutes, even if he is a world authority.

To see the typical Icelander, go to the Prikið café in Reykjavík. Here the men of Iceland come early, long before any of the shops have opened, to drink coffee. They sit in gloomy silence, their noses thrust deep into newspapers. Should anyone utter a sound he will receive the censorious stares usually reserved for those who sneeze in a library. In one corner sits an old man with a deer-stalker hat and a stiff moustache. He reads *Morgunblaðið*, the national daily, and sips coffee with an air of suspicion. Sit there all day and you will never see him leave. But if you should take your eyes off him for a moment, when you look again you will notice that he has been replaced by another, almost identical, man.

Public restraint is not matched by private diffidence. On a one-to-one basis the Icelander is talkative, the high esteem in which he holds himself breaking through the shyness. He will assume you wish to know his opinion about anything and everything. The fact that what he has to say may well be irrelevant to your circumstances, or the matter in hand, will be of little importance to him. He is an Icelander, you are an audience (however small), so you will be told. In the main his opinions will be worthwhile and interesting, but if they are not you will be in for a sorry time, for when the Icelander is boring he is very boring indeed.

Family Bonds

The Icelanders have a strong sense of family. Children help with the chores and despite increased affluence and satellite television there is a marked absence of the teenage conflict that affects other European nations. Perhaps this is because family life is less frantic. School hours are less lengthy than in the rest of Europe so there is more time for their social lives. Alternatively it could be that another old farming tradition lives on – that as long as the children behave marginally better than the sheep they will be left in peace.

However, with more and more mothers having (or choosing) to go out to work, children – never over-supervised or disciplined – are now free to roam at will, occasionally to the aggravation of others. One of the joys of Icelandic society is that, despite the annoyance this may cause, there is no fear that the kids will be harmed by anyone. Icelanders view societies in which children cannot play outside for fear of being molested as very sick indeed.

Although the trend is now for the old folk go into purpose built homes, until a few years ago it was quite usual for parents to move in with their children when old age made life difficult for them. It was not uncommon for a father to turn up on the doorstep of his daughter a day or two after the funeral of the mother. "Well," he would say, "here I am, where do you want me to sleep?"

No Hex on Sex

It is claimed that wherever foreign trawlers docked in Iceland many years ago there are now quite a few dark-haired, dark-eyed children. One place in the eastern fjords was even euphemistically called Congo as a result. This suggests that the Icelandic attitude to sex was always fairly liberal, sex being seen as a fun activity to be indulged in often, rather than something that was done with the lights off. Things haven't changed.

Liberal attitudes mean that the Icelandic man has never bothered to develop a series of 'chat up' lines. A straight-forward 'yes' or 'no' is all the conversation which occurs before the action starts. Whereas in most of the rest of Europe an invitation to 'come in for a coffee' is seen as a step on a road that might (but might not) lead to bed, in Iceland the coffee is served after, as a present for services rendered. As a result, Icelandic women like foreign males who spend half the night 'chatting them up' before moving on to the main event.

The local attitude to things sexual is epitomised by the Icelandic Museum of Phallology which has a display of 80 penises from over 30 species of mammal, together with a collection of related oddments. Though the museum does not yet a human specimen on show, the proprietor has been given the promise of one by a farmer who is over 80 – but not until it is no longer in regular use.

On Time Is Any Time

With instincts adapted from time immemorial to the whims of wind and sea, Icelanders are notoriously unpunctual. Their partners in the European Economic Area have come to regard this as a joke, for if a meeting was planned for 9 a.m., the Germans would arrive at 9 a.m. precisely and the Dutch at 8.40 a.m., but the Icelanders would turn up when they felt like it.

Shove While You Shop

On Saturday mornings there is a market in Reykjavík's custom's house. Stalls sell everything from motor bike bits to washing machines and the latest PCs. Junk and secondhand CDs are the most popular items. Icelanders flock to it, not just for the bargains on offer but for the opportunity it gives them to ignore queues and to barge and shout. It also allows them to finger the goods on offer, something to which they are strangely addicted.

Shops open at 10 a.m. Visitors who arrive in Iceland on a Friday assume this is because Friday night lasts until Saturday morning when the last of the revellers has gone home. In fact, the shops open at 10 a.m. every day to give those who are not working a leisurely start to the day.

A first-time visitor to Iceland could be forgiven for believing that every shop assistant in the land is called Hilda, for that, apparently, is what every Icelander calls out when he is in a shop. In fact, he is shouting "*Heyrðu*" which means "here", or "me next". Icelanders are the friendliest, most caring people you could hope to meet. But in a busy shop, don't get between an Icelander and the shop counter. He will ignore signs pleading for tolerance in public places in favour of the elbow. Shopping involves selecting your item and then pushing and shoving your way to the front of the throng at the counter, all the while shouting "*Heyrðu*". To an Icelander the idea of queuing, let alone the queue itself, is anathema, and he is seen at his worst in the state alcohol shops, especially on a Friday night.

In supermarkets the Icelander will wait in sullen line for his turn at the till, but only because the check-out areas have been constructed to be one person wide.

Manners

Meeting and Greeting

The Icelanders do not feel themselves bound by the conventions of polite society. They do not go in for formalities such as 'Good morning. How are you?'

Towns in Iceland are little more than villages and, as with all villages, most of the inhabitants know each other – indeed, as the new research shows, at some point over the last 10 or so generations they are probably related in some way, and so are either workmates, ex-school mates or 'uncles'. A quiet morning's shopping can turn into an epic journey through your past life. Just stopping to say hello can turn a quick trip into one requiring three days' leave from work. To control time loss, many Icelanders dispense with the usual conventions in an effort to maintain some privacy, but for those who do not put their heads down and ignore everyone they pass, elaborate rules of engagement exist. Ex-schoolmates who have not been seen for several years are not acknowledged unless they were particular friends who have moved from the area; a wave suffices for ex-workmates; and for those seen frequently, the standard handshake is used. For distant relatives a handshake – friendly but not too warm – and an enquiry about an old aunt are enough, though a hug might be required if they are rich. A hug and a coffee is much better if they are both rich and old.

The Icelanders used to be a more tactile race, the kissing of friends and relatives being the norm, but this gradually came to be seen as altogether too familiar and was stopped. However, the French habit of almost kissing both cheeks is becoming fashionable and has re-awakened their enthusiasm for touching.

Overseas Etiquette

The Icelander abroad will behave in one of two ways, or sometimes both, within the space of an hour. He can be an admirable ambassador for his country, even cleaning his hotel room before the maid arrives just in case she gets the idea that Icelanders are dirty or untidy, or he can be aggressive and demanding, even boorish.

Icelanders are consistently dismayed to discover that most foreigners neither know nor care where Iceland is. Impressed by their own linguistic skills, at home they will speak English to visitors, but as soon as they arrive in another country they will begin speaking Icelandic. With little chance of being understood, they can be as insulting as they wish without giving the slightest offence.

Conversation and Gestures

The Joy of the Jibe

A famous Icelandic poet used four-line verses to insult his contemporaries. The short verses were humorous, but cutting. In doing this the poet was not creating something new, but reinforcing a tradition that was centuries old. Even today there are gatherings where everybody has to invent and speak a four-line verse that humorously insults one or more of his fellow guests.

The essence of Icelandic conversation is the insult. Icelanders are born with a talent for it and use it with ease from an early age. Because of their farming and fishing ancestry the most telling jibes involve sheep and fish. It is a very serious matter to refer to someone as a sheep or a codhead. (In fact the Icelander is more likely to be offended by a suggestion that he is a sheep than that his father had a marked preference for ewes over women.) Equally potent is the suggestion that the Icelander is *púkalegur,* literally a peasant. You will be implying that he is lazy, stupid or uncultured. All these might be true, though laziness is far from being a national characteristic, but that is beside the point.

In conversation the Icelanders are wonderfully free of the English habit of meaning something other than what is actually said. Once a subject has been brought up for discussion, all aspects of it can be thoroughly and honestly explored, though this does not mean that all topics of conversation are allowed. Never ask how much an Icelander earns, and in no circumstances criticise his driving.

Despite the long tradition of swapping insults, there has never been an Icelandic tradition of gestures, rude or otherwise. So they import them. For instance, they have adopted the German one of tapping the side of the forehead to indicate stupidity. This is seen as genuinely offensive. If a driver intends making this sign to someone

29

who has cut in on him while driving in town, he will first scan the road ahead to ensure there is no set of traffic lights in sight.

Sense of Humour

A man was driving in the wilds of Iceland when his car suddenly stopped. He was not much of a mechanic, but in desperation he lifted up the bonnet and peered at the engine. He was shaking his head in exasperation when a voice beside him said, "It's your carburettor." Turning, he found himself face to face with a horse. He fled in fright, running over the brow of a nearby hill. Below he saw a farm and hurtled down to it. He banged on the door and the farmer let him in. He poured out the story to the farmer who sat impassively. When he had finished the farmer said, "What colour was the horse?" The man, stunned by the question, replied "Brown". "Ah," said the farmer, "take no notice of him. That one knows nothing about cars."

Another man was hauling in the trawl on a fishing boat when the trawl pulled violently and a cord severed two of his fingers. Horrified, the man rushed to the bridge to show the captain. "Look," he said, holding up his hand to reveal the bleeding stumps, "I've lost two fingers." The captain eyed him for a moment and then said "Not in here".

These are unusual Icelandic jokes in that everybody can appreciate them. Standard Icelandic humour is an acquired taste, one not normally shared by outsiders. For instance, the whole island rocked with laughter at the tale of an Icelandic woman who married a Turk. When the marriage failed, a long legal battle ensued which ended with the man taking their children off to Turkey. To get her revenge, the woman ate turkey for Christmas. (It can only be assumed that the joke is in the telling, or that the endless dark nights of winter do something to the brain cells.)

It has long been said that the Icelanders have no sense of humour at all. The grim-faced expression that is the norm (born of facing into the winter wind) rarely cracks into a smile. But Icelanders do have their own humour. It is derived from odd people and odd situations, with a special fondness for the surreal. As might be expected from a people with a long tradition of literacy, it also relies heavily on word play and spontaneity. In that sense it is akin to British humour, with puns and spoonerisms featuring strongly. A fine example of this is the description of two farms in the south of the country. For reasons lost in time one is called Grave. The other is called On the Edge of the Grave.

Much of the humour is kindly. In the Westmann Islands off the southern coast of Iceland, lived a man named Guðjón. During his twenties he moved to Reykjavík on three separate occasions each time failing to settle and returning home. From then on, until his death at the age of 81, he was affectionately known by his nickname, Guðjón *flækingur* (Guðjón the Wanderer).

Icelanders do have two groups of unfortunates whom they make the butt of acerbic humour. They tell jokes about the over-healthy Norwegians and their passion for sport. But mostly they joke about the inhabitants of Hafnarfjörður, a town a few miles from Reykjavík.

In Hafnarfjörður the inhabitants walk quietly past the pharmacies so as not to wake the sleeping pills; the refuse carts do 100 m.p.h. in case they are robbed; the children take ladders when they start at high school, and their parents take the same ladders shopping if they hear that prices are higher this week. The Icelandic expression for when the pavements are slippery is that they are covered in 'flying ice'. If the weather forecast predicts flying ice, Hafnies (people from Hafnarfjörður) sit outside in the cold all night, their eyes glued to the heavens for fear of missing this strange spectacle. Hafnies are also known as *gaflarars* – from *gafl* (gable) – because they are said to lean under the eaves of their roofs all day waiting for the world to come around the corner for an idle gossip.

The tone of the humour is such that the Hafnies tell the jokes too and have even turned them to their advantage. A Friends of Hafnarfjörður Society has been formed to promote the tall stories (no ladder required) and so gain commercial advantage, and the best Hafnie jokes are now told by Hafnies themselves.

Culture

It's a Continuing Saga

The great Icelandic sagas were written in the 12th, 13th and early 14th centuries and have been nourishing Icelandic culture ever since. Many people ask in all seriousness whether there would have been an Iceland without the sagas, such a powerful peg are they on which to hang nationhood. The Icelanders are well pleased that it was their Viking ancestors who produced these works, there being no equivalent from Denmark, Norway or Sweden. It is, however, a myth that today's Icelander can read the original texts without transcription, so difficult is the Gothic script.

As a result of constant re-evaluation, the sagas are as alive now as they were when they were written. Every day on prime-time radio there is a 15-minute reading from one of the sagas followed by a 15-minute discussion on the issues the passage raises. They are of such importance to the national culture that they form the basis of many a modern tale. Among the best is that of a truculent taxi driver who was stopped by four students on their way to a celebratory evening. Aware that he was the only car for miles around, he decided to make sure that they were worthy of his services. He said he would only take them if they were able to quote accurately the first line of *Njál's saga*. One of the students could, so he happily transported them. It is difficult to think of another European country in which a taxi driver could set such a puzzle and a student be able to answer it.

Everyone a Poet

An Icelandic maxim states that it is better to go barefoot than without books. More books are published in Iceland per head of population than in any other country, and they are of the highest quality. Although prices are outlandish, they sell in large quantities. So while it is said that if you offer a book to an Englishman for Christmas he will say 'No thanks, I've already got one', an Icelander will be thrilled at the prospect and spend the afternoon going through the shelves of all the local bookshops.

It is an Icelandic saying that if there is a topic in life then there must be a book on it. To make sure this is true, all Icelanders write, some of them profusely. Indeed, writing is a national pastime.

A major figure of the Icelandic literary scene is Halldór Laxness. A passage from his work *Heimsljós* (World Light) shows why he deserves such recognition:

'Where the glacier reaches up to the sky, the land ceases to be of this world and becomes a part of heaven; there can be no more sorrows there and therefore joy is no longer necessary, beauty alone rules, beyond any claims.'

The favourite medium is poetry, sometimes in the scaldic metre, a rhythm unique to Iceland largely because no-one else cares enough to use it. One aspect of the scaldic poem is its use of metaphor, the more complicated, and therefore unintelligible, the better. Thus no *skáld* (the term used for a scaldic poet) would dream of calling the sky the sky, not when he could call it 'the hero's hall', or of calling men men, when they could be 'the food of wolves'. A favourite theme is the retelling of the great epics, full of lyrical passages about the beauty of the sun going down over the fish-drying frames on cold, misty days in autumn. It is rumoured that one day Reykjavík will be adorned by a new statue raised in memory of the lone Icelander who never wrote a poem.

Art of the Matter

The visual arts are close to the heart of all Icelanders. Many people sculpt or paint in their spare time. It is as though the creativity of the Icelandic landscape is reflected in the creativity of its people. Like the Pompidou Centre in Paris, Iceland wears its bones on the outside, there being little vegetation to cover the geology. It also experiences over 20 earthquakes every day, and though most are minor, the landscape must never be taken for granted. This fluidity is reflected in Icelandic sculpture and painting.

Art is shared among the population rather than being maintained by an elite. Whereas in Britain it is often assumed that scientists do not understand artists and vice versa, in Iceland it is taken for granted that everyone is interested in art.

An Orchestral Feat

There are fine Icelandic composers, such as Jón Leifs and Atli Heimir Sveinsson and, most popular of all, Sigvaldi Kaldaóns, an impecunious country doctor who spent his spare time composing. Their music is played by the National Orchestra. The fact that Iceland has a National Orchestra is remarkable, not only because so small a country can afford to maintain one, but because enough people can be found to form one.

Eating and Drinking

The Icelanders are conservative eaters. As most of their food has to be imported, they have picked up Western habits and tastes. Breakfast is as likely to be cereal and coffee in Iceland as it is elsewhere, but older Icelanders still eat more traditional foods. For breakfast they will have *súrmjólk*, a form of sour milk, which looks and tastes like thin, light yogurt; or *Ristað brauð með osti*, hot toast served with butter, marmalade and thinly sliced cheese. (Iceland does not permit the importation of cheese, but as Icelanders like the taste of certain foreign cheeses, such as Stilton and Brie, they produce their own versions.)

For that important mid-morning snack to keep hunger pangs at bay, kiosks at bus stations and most bakeries sell rolls of exaggerated length and dubious content and cakes shaped like prehistoric ammonites. These huge buns are topped with sugar or a type of icing which is coloured either pink or dark brown.

Lunch is a sandwich or something equally light. The main meal of the day is eaten in the evening and for this fish and lamb are the favourites. Smoked lamb (*hangikjöt*) which has been hung over a lamb-dung fire is as close to the real flavour of the country as it is possible to get – it is said that the fire must be of lamb dung to give the taste an extra piquancy. This may be true. What is definitely true is that Icelandic lamb, smoked or not, is delicious.

Unusual fish dishes, such as cod cheeks, are tender and full of flavour. The Icelandic economy is virtually founded on cod, yet – apart from the cheeks – the Icelanders do not eat it. They consider it an ugly fish and do not eat ugly things. They prefer haddock which they claim is much better looking.

Fresh vegetables and fruit are shipped in all year round, though some vegetables, such as carrots, potatoes and cauliflowers, are grown locally.

Eating out is a favourite pastime, though an expensive

one. As in all cosmopolitan capital cities, it is possible to indulge in every kind of cuisine in Reykjavík – Italian, Indian, Chinese, Vietnamese. There is even a 'One Woman Vegetarian' restaurant.

One of the most fashionable places to eat is the Pearl. It sits on top of a giant hot water tank, built to store volcanically heated water for the central-heating systems of the city. The restaurant revolves, adding an extra dimension – indeed, several – to a meal. This is either ludicrous or brilliant fun, depending upon your point of view, but since it is too expensive to eat there, it doesn't really make any difference one way or the other.

Soured Seal Flipper and Pan-fried Puffin

Viking delicacies are claimed to be original and are very popular. One is rams' testicles pickled in whey. Others are congealed blood pudding, shark meat putrefied by being buried in the ground for several months, seal flipper soured in a way best left undefined, and boiled and pressed sheep's head. Icelanders wonder why the only authentic Viking restaurant in Reykjavík is not popular with visitors, while visitors wonder at the existence of even one.

Another Viking speciality can be found on the Westmann Islands. During the spring nesting season, the islanders collect puffins and puffin eggs. To collect the eggs, they throw themselves off the cliffs attached to thin ropes and swing about hundreds of feet above the lashing sea to reach the nests. Despite these antics having most clearly had their origins in hunger, the youth of the islands now practise the tradition as a sport, seeing who can travel the furthest, perform the most elegant arc, and survive. Adult puffins are netted on the cliff tops, an equally dangerous activity. Considering the effort involved, you would assume that puffin tastes like ambrosia. You would be mistaken. Pan-fried, boiled, braised or roasted –

nothing can make the bird taste like anything other than used sump oil.

Puffin is not so popular as dried fish. All over Iceland, but particularly in the north, fish of all types are hung out to dry on huge fish-drying frames like clothes on a line. They are left until they are as thin as paper and taste of old carpet. When the seagulls have lost interest in the fish, the Icelanders will begin to consider them ready to eat.

Coffee with a Kick

The traditional drink in Icelandic cafés is coffee which varies from just drinkable to lethal. Icelanders thrive on it, but visitors, especially those of a more delicate constitution, may find that two cups will bring on the shakes.

Many older Icelanders do not add sugar to their coffee but instead keep a *sykurmoli* (sugarcube) in their mouths while they are drinking, a habit which could go some way to explaining the silence of coffee drinkers. Although the young are adopting the Western habit of putting sugar in the cup, the word lives on in *Sykurmolarnir* – The Sugarcubes – one of the island's most popular rock groups. Björk Guðmundsdóttir, the elfin-like pop singer who won a British award as rock music's best, at one time was lead singer for this group.

All Kinds of Alcohol

It is said that God's gift to the Icelanders was a virgin land of incomparable beauty and diversity. The price modern Icelanders have to pay for the gift is the cost of alcohol.

Until 1989 beer was banned and even now is only available at state-controlled outlets at extortionate prices. The idea that prohibition would reduce drunkenness flew in the face of both logic and experience. In common with those other Vikings in Norway and Sweden, the Icelander long ago sorted out the problem of the long, dark winter months. The solution was straightforward: get drunk in September and don't sober up until late April.

Under prohibition, alcohol was available at certain times and places, one of which was when you were airborne. This meant that drinking started as the aeroplane was taxying to the end of the runway and stopped only when the doors opened at the flight's end. By then it was usually possible to pour the passengers out of the plane rather than have them disembark in the usual way.

Another effect of prohibition was that alcohol smuggling and illicit stills for bootleg drink were commonplace. The home-made version was so awful that large quantities of Coca-Cola had to be consumed to drown the taste. Habits die hard, and many older Icelanders still drink copious amounts of Coke, keeping the country's youth company.

Drinking is now legal, but controlled. Alcohol of any description can still only be bought at government liquor stores and is very expensive. Drinking is permitted in restaurants and bars where it is even more expensive. Making alcohol more accessible has reduced the amount consumed, but has had no effect on the nature of drinking. Icelanders do not understand social drinking. They drink purely to get drunk, a condition they seek with maximum enthusiasm at minimum expense. If it costs 10% less to get drunk on gin than on whisky, they will drink gin. Enquire whether taste is a consideration and they will look at you as though you are a fool. What could taste have to do with it?

As if to prove the point, the only truly Icelandic drink, *brennivín* (made from potatoes), tastes of nothing, cuts the throat like liquid emery paper and is known, with very good reason, as 'black death'. The Icelandic slang expression for drinking is 'to have a tear': clearly the power of the brew has long made the eyes water.

Since alcohol became legal, smuggling has been on the wane. This gladdens the heart of the coastguards, but is mourned by the media. For years the frequent chases and fights between smuggling seamen and officials provided great copy, as well as black eyes and other injuries. But because alcohol is so expensive, home brewing is on the increase, especially among the young, and there are frequent rumours of stills operating again in the wilds of lonely valleys.

The first of March is National Beer Day, celebrating the end of prohibition. The festivities take the form of a 24-hour-long binge largely indistinguishable from the celebrations on all other days.

Health

Life and Death

Icelanders have the highest life expectancy of any country in the world other than people in (the ex-Soviet State of) Georgia who are said to live regularly to 125. They put this down to their love of the outdoors – and there is an awful lot of outdoors to love – and their diet.

Not that long ago doctors were in short supply. The best help that could be obtained in country areas was the district nurse who was quite likely to be unavailable in spring because she was busy castrating that year's rams. A wise old family member would be all that was possible for consultation. As a result, most Icelanders are of the opinion that any ailment or pain is a minor problem, an inconvenience that will right itself in an hour or two, or a day at most. However, outside influences are putting this healthy aspect of Icelandic life into a new perspective. The young are beginning to believe that the rest of the world could well be right and that all minor ailments and pains are quite possibly to be symptomatic of something life threatening. Potions and pills are catching on.

Death is celebrated with a gathering of large numbers of family and friends. Though preferring to maintain their privacy most of the time, people come together for funerals in a spirit of warmth and fellow feeling.

Beautiful music and poetry form part of the ceremony at which the coffin is draped in the national flag. At the graveside, a poignant 16th-century psalm is sung about the life of man being as transitory as a little meadow flower which falls to the scythe:

> The sickle's blade descendeth
> Then in a moment's span
> Its bloom and beauty endeth
> So ends the life of man.

Death is becoming big business, people having realised that their funeral is the last possible status symbol. Increasingly, bands are hired to play the favourite music of the deceased and parties are organised. Absolved of all responsibility for the actions of the guests and the expense of it all, the corpses have the time of their lives.

Doctors and Dentists

The Icelanders claim that their high life expectancy is due in part to their excellent national health service. They pay a small fee when they go to a doctor, a bigger one to see a specialist.

The health service does not extend to dentists. This is understandable considering the quantity of sweets consumed by Icelanders of all ages. There is no insurance cover available for dentistry either. It is quite simple: you eat sweets, you get bad teeth, you go to the dentist and afterwards you settle his bill. The pain might be in your mouth, but you will certainly pay through the nose. The redeeming feature of this financial consideration is that it has promoted good oral hygiene, so that, despite all the sugar in their diet, the Icelanders are rarely obliged to fork out for fillings.

Condoms from Cabbies

Never having suffered from the puritanism of the Saxons, Icelanders fix their condom machines to the walls of bus stations rather than hiding them away in the 'Gents'. Even this has not been enough to prevent Aids obtaining a toe-hold. The latest attempt to reduce the spread of the disease has been the decision for taxi drivers to sell condoms. This is a sensible measure, though there is always the fear of the taxi driver demanding that one recites the first lines of *Njál's saga* before he parts with a packet.

Getting into Hot Water

Icelanders are both healthy and hygienic. The former they put down to the latter. Every town has an open-air swim-ming pool where all the year round people swim daily, the old folk early, the schoolchildren and parents later in the day. The water for the pools is volcanically heated so that even in winter, when the road outside is covered in snow and the wind is trying to move the water from the deep end to the shallow end, the Icelanders will still be steadily doing laps. It is a strange sight, steam from the hot water adding a surreal touch as the heads covered with frost bob relentlessly up and down.

Beside the pools steps go down into circular 'hot pots' in which the volcanic water varies from hot in the first pot to unbelievably hot in the last. A form of liquid sauna, bathers rest in these prior to and after swimming.

Before entering the pool, it is compulsory to shower and

wash. Free soap and shampoo are supplied and the shower water can be as hot as you can bear. Anyone attempting to enter the pool without showering will be met with the wrath of the attendant. The men's and the women's changing rooms employ an identical version: small and thin, caustic of tongue, and armed with a broom.

With all this showering and swimming Icelanders are very clean. The only slight drawback is that volcanic water smells of sulphur. It takes a while for outsiders to get used to the idea that very clean people can stink of rotten eggs.

Hygiene even extends to the eco-system. Any outsider wishing to fish in Iceland requires a certificate to prove to Icelandic officials that anything he intends putting into the water – waders, fishing rods, flies, etc. – has been sterilised. So even the salmon remain 'in the pink'.

Leisure and Pleasure

The most pleasurable thing the Icelanders can do is spend money, especially if they haven't got any. Gambling, however, does not much appeal to them. This is fortunate because, apart from the state lottery, gambling is only permitted by a charitable organisation or the University. However, there are many other things to spend money on.

Seeking the Sun

Given the fact that in Iceland bathing in the sea brings on hypothermia in seconds and sunbathing is likely to produce acres of gooseflesh long before it produces a tan, Icelanders dream of holidays in Spain and Florida. Foreign travel was difficult for so long that the novelty of going abroad has not worn off.

A Hut Above the Rest

All town-dwelling Icelanders have timber-built huts out in the middle of nowhere a couple of hours' drive from town. Their idea is to use them during spring and summer to escape the rigours of urban living, to rediscover their Icelandic roots, and to be at one with nature. However, as the town-dwelling Icelander lives in town precisely to avoid the rigours of the country that so plagued his grandfather and father, the huts are rarely visited. They are maintained solely to impress the neighbours.

Winter Sport

It is a myth that the Icelander is a hearty outdoor type who finds his country a rugged arena for pursuits which require large boots and a beard. When the snow scooter and glacier-driving fans have departed for home, the hardy few that are left are foreign skiers. Most Icelanders stay indoors during the winter, peering out anxiously every morning to see if spring has arrived. Or else do the sensible thing and go to Spain.

Summer Sport

The Icelanders will try their hand at anything. The newer the sport the better they like it, and if it requires a large amount of expensive equipment, they like it even more. Sport for children is well organised, and individuals do well. Several Icelanders play professional football in Germany, Scandinavia and Britain. In team games Iceland does about as well on the world stage as any medium-sized town would expect to do, though they do excel at handball.

The national sport is *glíma*, a form of wrestling. *Glíma* is unique to Iceland, though it has similarities to the wrestling practised in Western Samoa. No clear link has been established, and it does seem a long way to go for practice. The sport is very old and involves the wearing of traditional belts and much prancing about before the action starts.

Golf is currently the fastest growing sport in the country. There are few courses at the moment, but Iceland's position helps out for those unable to book a game. In summer the game can, and is, played all night as well as all day.

Car Crazy

People are always on the move, dropping the children off, going shopping, picking the children up again, going swimming. Reykjavík appears to have twice the number of vehicles that a city its size would normally have as Icelanders do everything by car.

But they also drive to such an extent that driving can be considered a leisure activity. Young Icelanders mix this dubious pleasure with that of drinking Coca-Cola, one hand on the steering wheel, the other holding aloft a can or bottle. They drive round the towns endlessly, a practice which has become so common it has been given a name – the *rúntur*, literally the round tour. When the *rúntur* became passé in Reykjavík, it moved on to Akureyri. This town being further north, the custom is for the occupants of the car, usually male, to wear clothes suitable for Californian beaches, turning the car's heater up full to compensate for the Icelandic temperature.

Icelanders drive all winter long, for in spite of its name, only 11% of Iceland is covered by permanent glaciers and the winters are harsh only in the remote centre of the country. No-one could live in the hostile interior, a place so lunar-like that N.A.S.A. took its astronauts there to train for landing on the moon.

Everyone lives on the coast, where the temperature rarely stays below freezing for very long periods, and snowfalls, although regular, are more of a nuisance than a hazard. Most drivers carry a spade in the boot as a precaution, and if they don't have a four-wheel drive vehicle, studded tyres, though not compulsory, are absolutely essential.

Four-wheel drive vehicles being a modern invention, all Icelanders must have one, so the roads are frequented by these huge machines, custom-fitted with massive wheels which threaten to drive over the top of any ordinary car daft enough to get in the way – like something straight out of *Terminator 2*.

In summer the latest craze is for towing huge 'folder homes', perhaps best described as collapsable caravans. These vast trailer-based houses are hauled all over the country for the satisfaction of the owners being able to erect them on some lonely spot for no particualr reason. Other road users are being driven to distraction as the cumbersome beasts take up all the road and drive very slowly. In winter the inhabitants will often be seen dragging horseboxes or vast trailers. These are for snow scooters, which a number of people delight in hauling out of town to some lonely spot, unloading with great effort and then driving aimlessly for an hour or so – just for the thrill of making tracks in the snow.

For some, even this thrill is inadequate, and there are those who fit even bigger wheels and tyres and drive off-road (although in view of the state of the roads this is something of a moot point), tackling snowfields, mountains and glaciers. This form of entertainment was invented by an Icelander, which is just as likely to be due to the fact that no other country could come up with anyone crazy enough to do so as it is to the quality of the northern intellect. Icelanders drive to places most people would not want to visit.

Infatuation with hi tech does not end with the vehicle itself. It will be kitted out with a telephone and a fax machine, a television and a CB radio. There is also likely to be a satellite navigation set. This is particularly handy if the vehicle happens to disappear into a glacial crevasse. The set, being accurate to just a few metres, will be able to tell the occupants almost precisely where they died.

Movies and Popcorn

Measured against the population there are four times as many cinemas in a big Icelandic town as there are in other countries. The Icelanders like the cinema, but not just for the films, which are mainly American or English and have sub-titles rather than being dubbed. Most of the audience follow the dialogue, but use the sub-titles to help out, which means they do not have to catch every spoken word. This is an advantage because the other reason for going to the cinema is to consume vast quantities of popcorn and to drink huge vats of Coca-Cola. As soon as the film starts, so does the noise, created by hundreds of munching jaws and the crackling of corn, followed by the slurping of hundreds of straws.

After about 45 minutes, right in the middle of a critical scene, the film stops and the lights go up. The consequence of the drinking is now apparent: the audience rises as one and flocks out. Ten minutes later everyone reappears, re-supplied with large containers, and the whole procedure starts again.

Partying the Night Away

The Icelanders are great ones for entertainment. Centuries of making their own amusement in turf huts during the long dark winters have left them in permanent need of company. As a result there is a huge number of things to do and places to go in the towns – theatres, clubs for all kinds of music, discos, restaurants.

For the committed drinker the weekend starts on Friday afternoon at home. It starts there because it is

cheaper to drink at home than in a bar. The rule, therefore, is to drink heavily at home, going out just to finish
the job off in the company of a few like-minded people.

For the rest of the population the weekend starts at
midnight, none of the clubs closing before 3 a.m., when
everybody moves on to a party. Dancing was outlawed
by the Danes who believed that the high level of illegitimate births in Iceland was attributable to it. After Home
Rule had been established, the ban was lifted. The
Icelanders, being a more intelligent people, had worked
out that dancing was not the cause.

Old Time Entertainment

A famous old Icelandic book of games for all the family
includes one that involved lying people down on their
backs, putting a coin on their nose, and laughing at the
faces they pulled as they tried to flick the coin off without
using their hands. Another game was a race between two
groups of four people who passed eggs to one another
using spoons held in the mouth. Again, no hands were
allowed, and the eggs were real. No wonder Icelanders
were grateful when television arrived.

Ads for Fads

American television was available at an early stage of
broadcasting history in Iceland. The populace was appalled
by the crassness of the advertisements, and since none of
the advertised goods was actually for sale in Iceland, they
were able to reinforce their cultural snobbery by noting
frequently and at length that they were far too intelligent
to be hoodwinked by such rubbish.

However, when the single Icelandic television channel
offered advertising, one company used the saturation
technique to sell a foot massager. It was allegedly both

useless and unnecessary, but by the end of the campaign it is estimated that 50% of Icelandic houses had one and that no-one had used it more than once.

At one time Iceland's own channel was not screened on Thursdays nor for the whole of July so that the producers and presenters could enjoy a day off and take a summer holiday. Few other countries in the world would tolerate such a situation. Now it broadcasts every day of every month, and even at breakfast-time.

The audience is becoming more sophisticated and the most popular show is a satirical news quiz. It just tops the other favourite which is a fun-and-games show composed of a mixture of candid camera situations, chat, talent contest and pantomime. Due to the small size of the population, almost every Icelander will appear on the show at some time. Why else would people watch?

Custom and Tradition

Sons and Dóttirs

The majority of Icelandic Christian names are as old as the sagas. There you find Harald of the Grey Cape and Bork Blue Tooth Beard. Today it is possible to have a drink with Stone, son of Wolf (Steinn Úlfsson), or with Eagle, son of Bear (Örn Björnsson). And, what is more, it is possible to do so without having your head cleaved in twain and your wife broached.

Icelanders take great pride in being the only Viking country to maintain patronyms, the use of the father's given name as the child's surname. The usage produces the oddity of a standard nuclear family of father, mother, son and daughter having four different surnames. If Pétur, the son of Björn, marries Guðrún, daughter of Vilhjálmur, and they have two children, Marta and Einar, at a

European hotel the family will sign in as Pétur Björnsson, Guðrún Vilhjálmsdóttir, Marta Pétursdóttir and Einar Pétursson. Hotel receptionists have been known to weep.

The use of patronyms has the potential to make the telephone directory one of the most difficult books in the world to follow. To counter the problem, it lists everybody by both Christian and surnames. But this is only a partial solution as there is a limited number of Christian names so there are always several people with the same names. The next obvious addition would be the address, so here the Icelanders add the profession of the person. Only then is the address given. Almost as an afterthought the telephone number is listed, although by the time they have waded through all the earlier information most folk have forgotten why they wanted to make the call.

The Nobel prizewinning author, Halldór Laxness, was one of a very small number of Icelanders who took a European-style surname. In others this would be looked down on as an affectation. In his case it was acceptable because he is looked upon as a genius.

The Need to Knit

Thirty years ago knitting would have rated a score as high on the national obsession scale as politics and the weather. In country areas it still does, but the town dwellers have long since stopped indulging in what they perceive as a yokel's pursuit, in public at least. Many of Iceland's excellent young artists are women who have put down their knitting needles and taken up paint brushes.

Both men and women knitted. They made blankets from knitted triangles, gloves with fingers but without seams (a skill which still attracts the admiration of the knowledgeable), sweaters, anything and everything to keep out winter's chills. Stories of obsessional knitting are legion. Cow and sheep herders knitted as they walked across Iceland's rugged landscape. Farmers' wives were even said to have knitted while they made love.

A beautiful product of all this endeavour is the *lopi,* the sweater with the characteristic half-moon of intricate patterning around the neck. Those made for sale to visitors tend to be made with the addition of soft imported wool, because the wool from Icelandic sheep (which have long guard hairs to keep out winter's chills) is coarse. The Icelanders call articles knitted from it *stingubolur,* literally 'underwear that pierces', because it is so prickly.

Spring Hop

The earliest Icelanders had a miserable time during the five months of winter, even more miserable than their modern compatriots. To keep themselves sane they had regular festivals, the most important being the midwinter *þorrablót* named after the ancient Norse month of *Þorri.* This began with a week of feasting during the third week of January, and by the time the celebrations were over in the third week of February, only a few weeks of winter remained, the days were rapidly getting longer, and spring was on its way.

It became customary for Icelanders to welcome *Þorri* by putting only one leg into their trousers and hopping barefoot around the yard. The church authorities tried to end the festival (not least, perhaps, to avoid half Iceland's congregations hobbling into church on crutches as a result of a single frost-bitten foot), but it was revived under Danish rule as a symbol of nationalism. Today it is enthusiastically celebrated for much the same reason that the earliest settlers enjoyed it. Traditional foods are eaten and a quantity of drink consumed. The hopping is no longer compulsory, but is quite likely to occur at those gatherings where sufficient lubrication has been provided to remove all inhibitions.

Rash Wednesday

In a festival that mixes the pagan past and the Christian present, on Ash Wednesday all Icelandic children put on fancy dress and spend the day trying to humiliate adults.

Quite the weirdest aspect of the festival is *kattarslagur* in which the children use home-made swords or clubs to sever a rope suspended through a barrel. Not so long ago, for reasons lost in the mists of time, a dead cat was hung on the end of the rope. Nowadays, to the relief of all concerned, and most especially the Icelandic cat population, a fluffy toy hangs from the rope.

Ash Wednesday is preceded by Bun Day, the Icelandic equivalent of Shrove Tuesday. This sounds normal enough, but even this Icelandic festival includes the bizarre, the custom being to win a bun for having hit someone across the backside with a stick before he or she has got out of bed.

Government and Bureaucracy

Trading Insults

Being the first nation in the world to elect a woman as head of state swells the national chest, but the Icelander's attitude towards the position of president is in marked contrast to that afforded to other politicians.

Since they view politics as the province of the stupid and corrupt, they hold all politicians in low esteem and every couple of years give them the opportunity of finding a decent way of earning a living by the straight-forward expedient of kicking them out. Unfortunately some politicians are given directorships of the National Bank when they lose office, a fact that annoys the voters who did not have that in mind at all. One irate Icelander referred to the National Bank as the kindergarten for unloved politicians. This caused great offence and, therefore, great amusement.

Having no national rude gesture, the people have to content themselves with publicly humiliating those they wish to offend. The greatest humiliations are reserved for their politicians, the very greatest for those who attain the highest offices. You can be sure that if a politician has an offensive nickname, he is someone who has been singled out for high office. If it is really offensive, he is probably the prime minister.

Newspapers reflect the nation's feeling about all politicians; in fact it is generally assumed that reporters are under an obligation to be insulting. However, the source of their ire is not that politicians are evil or lead immoral lives, but that they are inept and stupid. By contrast, those who are insulted by politicians are shocked. It is as though the ducks had started to shoot back. A television producer with a string of deeply offensive political shows to his credit was insulted – as he saw it – by a government minister. With cries of outrage, he declared his intention of supporting libel cases for those who found themselves in a similar position, and promptly formed the Association of People Who Have Been Insulted By Politicians.

Some politicians are a satirist's dream. Prime Minister David Oddsson is small and round, and has a mop of curly hair. A savage attack suggested that the hair and certain features could be traced to a Caribbean influence. This was emphatically denied, family lines back to the 9th century being offered for public scrutiny. The whole debate was irrelevant to politics but was hugely enjoyed, the more so since the prime minister in his student days had taken part in a radio comedy show which specialised in being spiteful to politicians.

Left, Right and Centre

Iceland has 63 members of parliament drawn from a handful of main parties. The Independence Party, the party with the largest number of seats, holds power in a moderately right-wing coalition with the Progressives.

The ten-man coalition cabinet has been rightish of centre for more years than can be remembered, though this seems to matter little to the populace who believe that the differences between a useless right-wing government and a useless left-wing government are frequently overstated in other countries. Yet, interestingly, they invariably elect a leftish President in order to give the system some sort of balance.

A poll claimed that despite a leftward trend in politics there were just three Communists in the country. One was the gum-chewing presenter of Iceland's best radio jazz programme. The second was the keeper of the most northerly lighthouse, a man known as Óli the Commie, who is rumoured to have a picture of Stalin on the wall. The third person was not named for fear of libel action.

The women of Iceland formed a party, the Women's List, but the dominance of the ruling party led to its break-up and the majority formed an alliance with another large party to try to counteract the Independence Party.

Because the Independence Party has led governments and coalitions since 1904, rumours of corruption, patronage and nepotism are rife. These are widely believed to exist, though there has never been a formal investigation. With a sigh and a shake of the head, the Icelanders just accept the situation, together with the somewhat obvious gerrymandering of constituencies that often goes on before elections. This may go some way towards explaining both the savageness of the satire and the general attitude that it is best to get on with having a good time before the madmen in power mess it all up.

The Uncivil Civil Service

The Civil Service, having been around for the same length of time as the coalition, looks more like the government than the government does. Its employees often behave that way too, subverting democracy by obstructing progress when they disagree with proposals of the elected members, an attitude which leads to the suggestion that Iceland could successfully do away with a layer of government, namely the elected layer.

Even when the government has voted in favour of something, it can sometimes be difficult to get it done. There will be some junior clerk in some obscure ministry who does not like the idea. Once he has halted progress, the whole stubborn machinery of the Civil Service will come in on his side and the idea will be lost in a welter of red tape. The fact that something is official policy is of no consequence if it does not happen to be Civil Service policy.

Systems

More Rut Than Road

Iceland is big. It is a bit bigger than Ireland, almost three times the size of Belgium, and the same size as Kentucky. To drive around it takes days.

In part this is due to the fact that, because of the harsh climate, roads are at best poor and at worst dreadful. Those travelling to *þingvellir,* site of the world's oldest parliament, will find the road good, being metalled all the way there and around the bend. *Þingvellir* is set in a raised circle of grass beside a volcanic rift, and is an almost compulsory item on the itinerary of every Icelandic tour company. The vast majority go no further than this, so do not know that beyond the next bend the road reverts to the Icelandic norm – a gravel track that frequently degenerates into a gravel track interspersed with pot holes. A journey takes on epic proportions as you weave between the holes, desperately hoping for a length of road that will not interfere with your digestion.

Periodically a landslip, caused by summer rain, winter snow, or volcanic activity, will inundate the road. The Icelanders remain unfazed by this, merely calling out a steam roller to flatten the soil heap and then driving on the top. As a result in some places the road lies several feet above the surrounding land.

At intervals a curious sign – *blindhæð* – indicates that the next section should be driven with care as the road is about to go over a hump. Despite the fact that in this sparsely populated country it is possible to drive all day without actually getting anywhere or meeting anyone, the hump will always be concealing the one car that is coming in the opposite direction.

To help the poorly sighted at pedestrian crossings in Reykjavík, a ticking noise has been added to the green 'walk' signal. The noise is all but inaudible, but when someone does hear it, they usually assume that one of the hidden people has become trapped inside the device and is knocking to be let out. By the time the confusion is over the 'walk' light has changed to red.

Public Transport

Iceland has an excellent internal air service. Keflavík is probably the most beautiful airport in the world and certainly the only one built on a piece of land obtained a thousand years ago in exchange for an embroidered cloak.

The bus system is equally efficient. Given a few weeks one can travel all the way around the island, stopping off to see things and then hopping back on the bus again. It can pose a problem though, when on a Monday morning the reply to the question "When is the next bus?" is "Wednesday afternoon". Bus stops are not well equipped for those who decide to wait.

You can't catch a train because there aren't any.

Powered by Nature

In spite of having no coal or oil, the Icelanders have an almost perfect power system, being blessed with lashings of natural hot water. Some water is used to generate electricity, and more is used to provide central-heating systems in the houses. The water is metered and paid for by the gallon.

Even the waste water – which is still quite warm – is utilised, pipes being run under the pavements to melt the winter's snow and ice. This system is not organised by the town councils, so individual householders have to pay for the pipes to be installed. It is therefore possible to walk along a street that has a snow heap requiring moun-taineering skills, then a section of clean, wet pavement, then a tricky iced section where pipes do not exist, and then another snow mountain. It pays to be alert.

Emergency Services

There is a very efficient coastguard service which more or less stands in for army, navy and air force. During the Cod Wars a coastguard boat with a machine gun mounted on the front was more than a match for the British Royal Navy.

As nothing seems to burn down during the Icelandic winter, the fire brigade spends its time making savings for the health service. This the firemen do by removing icicles the size of the Sword of Damocles which hang menacingly from the gutterings of high buildings.

In the summer months the brigade deals with a few fires. It cannot fill in its time by rescuing the odd cat stuck in a tree. There are no trees for it to get stuck in.

Distant Degrees

Formal education starts when children are six, though there are plenty of pre-school groups that take children from three years old for the day or half-day. Compulsory schooling lasts from six to 16, after which there is high school until the age of 20.

At this stage many youngsters either go abroad or go on to university. There are two universities, in Reykjavík and Akureyri, but being a small country means that Iceland does not have the resources to cover all subjects. So if you want to study subjects such as architecture or post-graduate medicine you must go abroad, and a staggering number of students do so.

Overseas travel has advantages and disadvantages. On the one hand, returning students bring a cosmopolitan element to Iceland. Two students from America who have studied the same discipline together in Europe, might live 3,000 miles apart and never see or hear of each other again after they get home, but Icelanders in a similar situation may live in adjacent streets and meet up in the supermarket.

On the other hand, returning students can see their homeland as small and parochial and find it wanting.

Law and Order

It's a Fair Cop

The police, who are known as *löggan*, a shortened form of the Icelandic for 'servant of the law', are liked. Little boys want to grow up to be policemen, though this may have something to do with their being unable to be train drivers. Parents do not object since the police are seen as friendly and by no means the hard hand of the state.

The police are hot on speeding and all cop cars are fitted with radar speed guns. They are even hotter on drink-driving. The merest suspicion of alcohol in a driver's blood and he is in very hot water indeed.

The story is told of a group of men enjoying a meal in a Reykjavík restaurant when a drunk, lurching towards the door, stole a coat belonging to one of them. The group pursued him and stopped a passing police car so that he could be arrested. The drunk, the coat and the coat's owner were taken to the police station where the drunk was put in a cell and the coat-owner assisted in filling out the necessary forms. That completed, the man asked what would happen to the drunk.

"Well," said the policeman in charge, "would you like to go into the cell and knock him about a bit?"
"What?" said the man, shocked by the suggestion, "he's twice the size of me."
"Hmm," said the policeman, "you have a point. Would you like us to go in first and mollify him a little?"

Every Icelander would deny this tale of course, though only after he had told it. But it illustrates some basics about Icelandic justice which is rooted in the old Viking idea of natural justice administered by policemen who are on the side of the injured party.

58

Disorderly Conduct

Most crime is drink-related, the Icelanders being aggressive when they have had too much to drink. Window breaking is popular, particularly with Iceland's glaziers, as a stroll downtown on a Sunday morning will demonstrate.

Occasionally a drunken brawl results in a death and someone is charged with manslaughter. Murder is very unusual, so rare, in fact, that a murder in the north of the country in the early 19th century still attracts debate. When another took place in 1990, the *löggan* called in a detective from Hamburg because they felt so out of their depth. In the nature of finding a way of making cash from virtually any situation, the guilty party has written a best-selling book on salmon fishing.

The only serious white-collar crime is tax evasion which costs the state millions every year, but most Icelanders show little concern as the state is seen as fair game. If someone is caught it is felt to be more bad luck than justice.

Business

There is a close association between big business and the leading political party. It is seen as too close, especially when politicians become spokesmen for the businesses, and when the directors of the leading banks (very high earners) are political appointees.

People are strong believers in the existence of the *Kolkrabbi* (Octopus), an organisation (probably informal but, as always with these things, who knows?) of the country's 14 leading families who control the major businesses and have members within the government. The sighting of two of them together in a car is usually accompanied by sneering comments about meetings of the Octopus, though as with all other political scandals the Icelanders much prefer sarcasm and insults to real action.

The Icelanders also believe that the next largest political party and another group of influential men (chiefly rich farmers) form the Squid. Depending on the composition of the current coalition, the Octopus and the Squid will either be at daggers drawn or enjoying cosy lunches to their mutual advantage, but whichever way it is the ordinary Icelander will derive little benefit. Icelanders hope that the recent creation of an Icelandic stock market will curb the power of these alliances.

Weak trades unions have given businessmen the edge in wage negotiations, while centuries of history have bred an independence of mind. This combination means that most Icelanders aspire to be their own bosses, and many set up businesses, starting small and usually getting smaller before they disappear. If the Taiwanese invent battery-operated back scratchers, you can rest assured that by the end of the first week of production an Icelander will have formed a business to import them. Money will be borrowed, premises hired and staff employed but more often than not to no avail, the bottom having falling out of the back scratcher market within two weeks. One might imagine that the Icelanders, being an intelligent race, would learn from their mistakes. But their faith in economists and their own abilities is without limits.

The government approves of all this commerce, one minister having been tempted to state that the number of bankruptcies in the country was a measure of its economic health. This is an interesting view and one that would certainly be appreciated by the importer of several thousand back scratchers.

The exceptions to the rules of Icelandic economics are

the fishermen. They are the highest-paid workers in the country, earning five times the salary of a university lecturer. They have tax concessions as well, and an attempt by the government to reduce these was followed by a fishermen's march to the parliament building. Such direct action was so unusual and shocking that the government backed down immediately.

Language and Ideas

The Dane, Rasmus Christian Rask, claimed in the early 19th century that he had learned Icelandic in order to be able to think. This was a wonderful, some would even say moving, compliment. But he also predicted that Icelandic would be dead in 100 years, killed off by Danish, the language of the island's rulers. But the Danish rulers did not ban Icelandic (merely ignored it) and the language survived. Danish was the language of commerce and government. It was also the language of snobbery, used by the Icelandic 'gentry'. It is ironical that the Icelanders' dislike of pretension and the working man's dislike of the upper class saved the language from extinction.

Similar predictions are now being made about the death of Icelandic at the hands of English. The particular problem is the number of English-speakers who come to Iceland to study, drawn by its uniqueness. If a class has ten Icelanders and one non-Icelandic-speaking foreigner then the lecture will be given in English. The Icelanders have a term for this – 'Ignorance is Strength' – which illuminates their concern for their language.

To the list of obsessions another could have been added – Icelandic. Icelandic is an exotic language based on an alphabet with 33 letters, the extra ones being extremely picturesque and completely unpronounceable.

A poem in Icelandic by William Jón Holm entitled The Icelandic Language, expresses it thus:

In an airconditioned room you cannot understand the
    grammar of this language,
The whirring machine drowns out the soft vowels,
But you can hear these vowels in the mountain wind
And in heavy seas breaking over the hull of a small boat.
Old ladies can wind their long hair in this language
And can hum, and knit, and make pancakes.
But you cannot have a cocktail party in this language
And say witty things standing up with a drink in your hand.
You must sit down to speak this language,
It is so heavy you can't be polite or chatter in it.
For once you have begun a sentence, the whole course of
    your life is laid out before you,
Every foolish mistake is clear, every failure, every grief,
Moving around the inflections from case to case and gender
    to gender,
The vowels changing and darkening, the consonants soft-
    ening on the tongue
Till they are the sound of a gull's wings fluttering
As he flies out of the wake of a small boat drifting out to
    open water.

The Icelanders are as proud of their language as they are of their country and protect it fiercely from what they view as external invasion. Committees set up for its protection go to great lengths to avoid absorbing foreign words. When a new concept or invention is imported into Iceland, the relevant committee sets about producing an Icelandic equivalent. The sagas are scoured for a word no longer in common usage that can be pressed into service. To avoid 'telephone' the word *sími* was dredged up, an ancient word for a thread. 'Satellite' presented a problem, but *gervitungl* was manufactured from the words for 'artificial' and 'moon'. Television is called *sjónvarp*, combining the words for seeing and casting out (as in fishing), while computer combines *tala* – the word for number – and *völva* – soothsayer or prophetess – to create *tölva*. Despite the concocted nature of these words and the Icelanders' love of the very latest technology, they are readily accepted and used by everyone.

Very occasionally something comes along that creates a real problem: what to do, for instance, with 'intercontinental ballistic missile'? The sagas did not offer a word for 'spear thrown from a great distance' so a new one had to be made up which means 'long distance fiery flying thing'. Most Icelanders just say ICBM.

No Icelandic words inhabit the international lexicon, though the Icelanders do lay claim to several of Viking origin that have found their way into English. Best of all they like *berserk*, probably deriving from 'bear-skin' and used as a term for warriors who fought with the strength of ten men and were immune to pain. It is likely that berserkers were totally intoxicated, a condition much favoured by the population.

The Icelanders are pleased to the point of embarrassment if a foreigner learns their language. At one time it was discovered that a Georgian lawyer had taught himself Icelandic. He did not know any Icelanders and had done it purely for his own enjoyment, translating a quantity of Icelandic literature into his own language. The Icelanders were so impressed and grateful, they invited the man and his wife to Iceland at the country's expense, and wined and dined them for the entire two months.

The Author

Richard Sale was born in England's West Country – reason enough to feel sympathy with all minorities who speak with strange tongues.

Being quite good at sums he took a degree in theoretical physics and a PhD in astrophysics, and then sought a job in glaciology in order to be nearer his first great loves, snow and ice. He is now a travel writer, specialising in wilderness areas, most particularly the Arctic.

He fell in love with Iceland the first time he saw it – barely, through the fine rain that was falling – and has been going there, summer and winter, ever since. He is constantly frustrated by its weather and endlessly fascinated by its mixture of landscapes, its bird life and its people (though not always in that order).

He would like to thank several Icelandic friends for their (sometimes inadvertent) assistance with this book. Sadly, none of them is willing to be identified.